What Ship is NOT a Ship?

Harriet Ziefert   *illustrated by* Josée Masse

BLUE  APPLE

For Lori —H.Z.

To my wonderful sisters-in-law, Anne, Marie and Hélène—J.M.

Text copyright © 2014 by Harriet Ziefert
Illustrations copyright © 2014 by Josée Masse
Art direction and design by Elliot Kreloff
All rights reserved/CIP data is available.
Published in the United States 2014 by
🍎 Blue Apple Books, 515 Valley Street,
Maplewood, NJ 07040
www.blueapplebooks.com

First Edition
Printed in China 09/14
ISBN: 978-1-60905-447-2
1 3 5 7 9 10 8 6 4 2

A panda bear is a bear.

A brown bear is a bear.

A polar bear is a bear.

bear: a large, heavy animal with shaggy hair and a small tail that eats both plants and meat

What bear is NOT a bear?

A woolly bear is NOT a bear!

What is a woolly bear?
a fuzzy caterpillar
that will become a tiger moth

An apple pie is a pie.

A pumpkin pie is a pie.

A key lime pie is a pie.

pie: a dish consisting of
a pastry crust and a filling

What pie is NOT a pie?

A magpie is NOT a pie!

What is a magpie?

a bird with a long tail,
white markings on its feathers,
and a noisy, chattering call

A racehorse is a horse.

A rocking horse is a horse.

A workhorse is a horse.

horse: a hoofed, grazing animal used for riding and for carrying and pulling loads

What horse is NOT a horse?

A seahorse is NOT a horse!

What is a seahorse?

a small sea creature with bony plates
covering its body that swims upright

A baseball hat is a hat.

A ski hat is a hat.

A hard hat is a hat.

A cowboy hat is a hat.

hat: a shaped covering for the head worn for warmth, as a fashion item, or as part of a uniform

What hat is NOT a hat?

A hi-hat
is NOT a hat!

What is a hi-hat?
foot-operated cymbals,
part of a drum set

A sheepdog is a dog.

A bulldog is a dog.

A hound dog is a dog.

dog: a domesticated animal that is related to the wolf, eats meat, has a strong sense of smell, and communicates by barking, howling, or whining

What dog is NOT a dog?

A hot dog is NOT a dog!

What is a hot dog?
a cooked sausage, sometimes called a frankfurter

What frog is NOT a frog?

frog: a tailless animal with a short body, moist, smooth skin, and very long hind legs for leaping

A game of leapfrog is NOT a frog!

What is leapfrog?

a game in which one player bends over while the other players take turns jumping over the person crouching down

kid's bedroom

hall

living room

What room is NOT a room?

room: a part of the inside of a building that is separated by walls

bathroom

parent's bedroom

kitchen

A mushroom is NOT a room!

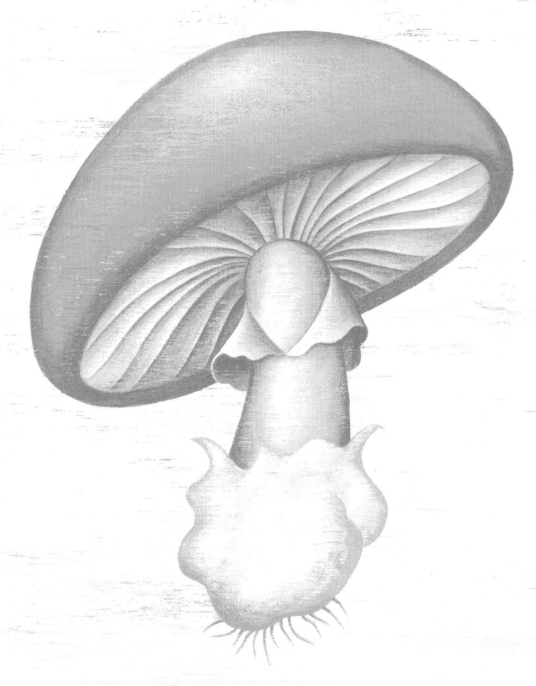

What is a mushroom?

a fungus with a stalk and a cap that looks like a small umbrella;
some kinds of mushrooms can be eaten, while other kinds are poisonous

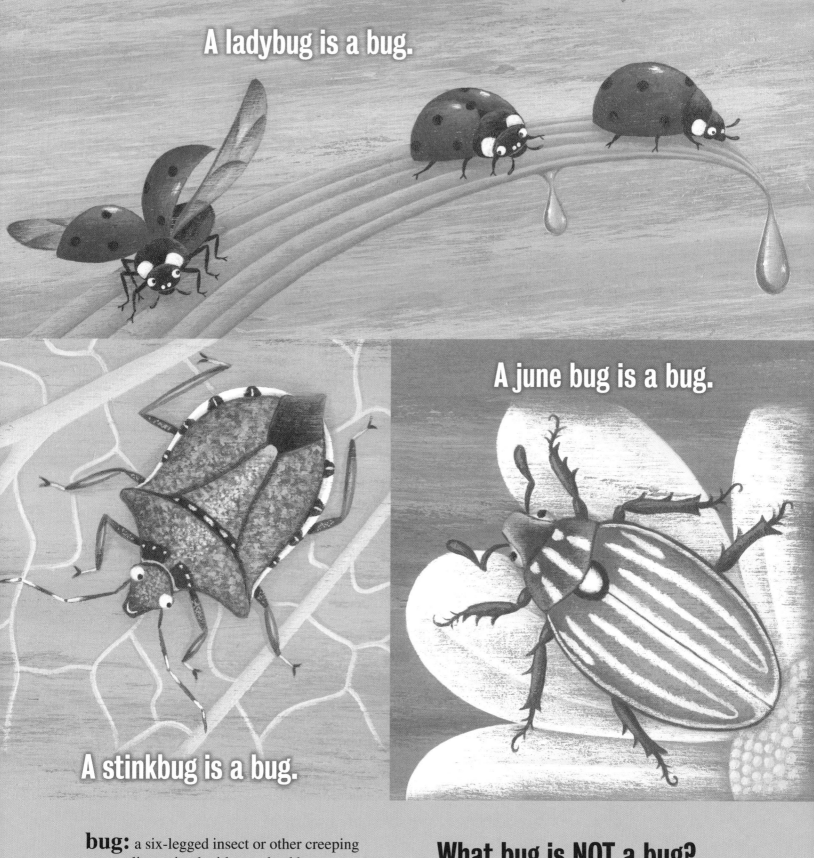

A ladybug is a bug.

A june bug is a bug.

A stinkbug is a bug.

bug: a six-legged insect or other creeping or crawling animal without a backbone

What bug is NOT a bug?

A litterbug is NOT a bug!

What is a litterbug?

someone who throws waste paper or other trash on streets, roadsides, or other public places

What key is   NOT a key?

key: a small piece of shaped
metal used open or close a lock

A monkey is NOT a key!

What is a monkey?
a small, long-tailed primate that lives in warm regions

A handsaw is a saw.

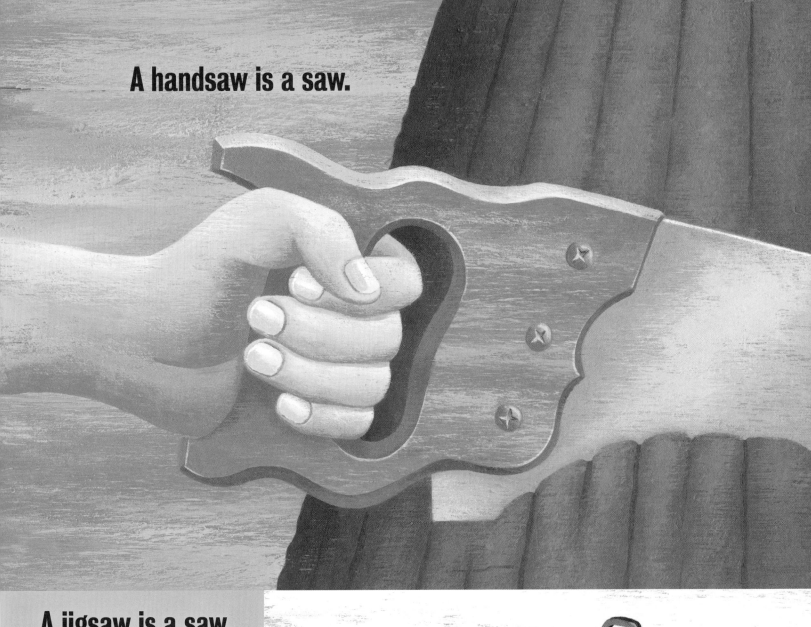

A jigsaw is a saw.

A chain saw is a saw.

saw: a tool with a tooth-edged blade used to cut hard material

What saw is NOT a saw?

A seesaw is NOT a saw!

What is a seesaw?
a plank balanced in the middle so that one end
goes up as the other goes down

A cargo ship is a ship.

What ship is NOT a ship?

**A sailing ship
is a ship.**

A battleship is a ship.

ship: a large boat for transporting people or goods by sea

Friendship is NOT a ship!

What bird is NOT a bird? Play the guessing game!

A blackbird is a bird.
A catbird is a bird.
A hummingbird is a bird.

What bird is NOT a bird?

An earring is a ring.
A wedding ring is a ring.
A toe ring is a ring.

What ring is NOT a ring?

A mealworm is a worm.
An earthworm is a worm.
A tapeworm is a worm.

What worm is NOT a worm?

A bumblebee is a bee.
A honeybee is a bee.
A queen bee is a bee.

What bee is NOT a bee?

A spotted hog is a hog.
A warthog is a hog.
A black hog is a hog.

What hog is NOT a hog?

A bunk bed is a bed.
A water bed is a bed.
A daybed is a bed.

What bed is NOT a bed?

A cow's horn is a horn.
A goat's horn is a horn.
A unicorn's horn is a horn.

What horn is NOT a horn?

A teacup is a cup.
A coffee cup is a cup.
An egg cup is a cup.

What cup is NOT a cup?

A jawbone is a bone.
A collarbone is a bone.
A chicken bone is a bone.

What bone is NOT a bone?

A fishnet is a net.
A butterfly net is a net.
A hairnet is a net.

What net is NOT a net?

A baseball is a ball.
A tennis ball is a ball.
A meatball is a ball.

What ball is NOT a ball?

To find the answers,
search for *What Ship Is Not a Ship?* at:
www.blueapplebooks.com.

**Can you think of a few puzzles
to stump your friends and teachers?**